bloom little flower

Irene Limon

BookLeaf Publishing

Presentation by *BookLeaf Publishing*

Web: www.bookleafpub.com

E-mail: info@bookleafpub.com

ISBN: 9789357442718

First edition 2023

Dedicated to my loving husband Joseph, my two beautiful children Aurora and Rowan. I cherish every moment with you!

bloom little flower

be still little one,
stay safe in my arms.
now reach for the sun,
avoid every harm.
bloom like no one is watching!

Earth

soil solidified,
quiet clashing Titans rise,
all is still again.

She is solid ground,
our Mother in life and death,
all return some day.

Water

forever dancing,
playful, harsh, unforgiving
eternal movement.

fluid, in motion
constant channels move our world,
wash away my pain.

Air

rush past, Silent One
always there but never Seen.
secrets/ screams alike.

soft caress, my heart
feels you there, a shadow near
whispers, "always mine"

Fire

sparks, colors Ignite
engulf thy passions in Red
She consumes, then kills.

slick quick licks become
fast raging pain, Destruction
a new world of ashes.

singing bee

tell me your sticky secrets,
sing them to me Bee.
drip like honey,
hum them, thoughts
in a floral melody.
please will you sing them
sweetly little Bee.

Human

being Human is kind of like...
Love, sweet tenderness
cuddles, dreams & kisses.
squishy Feelings
melted together with complication.
something missing in between
each laugh, each hug, each other.
Curiosity, endless like stars
asking, begging to be Seen.
Shining bright,
a slow burn builds.
Colliding realities
create more... Love.
Human.

roots

Deep, deep, deep
deep down.
Solid connection
Flowing toxicity
through veins of love.
Love to give,
love to take,
love to hurt,
love to hate...
These roots are mine
not mine alone.
Ours.
Past loves, past lives, past mistakes
always there.
Through years
twisted, entangled,
deep deep down,
inside.

little deaths

dormant soul, darkness
infinite slumber, alive
Reborn, flesh & wild

Cosmic Gift

the gift of universal love,
equivalent to eternal pain
naive affections present
deep hollow hearts.
a child born of heartache,
fill the void.
glare into the sun,
let flames singe reality.
explode ecstasy to the mass,
nothing but stardust...

balance

cruelty & kindness
harmony in symmetry
our Euphoric bliss

water me please

I see you
sitting there.
My muse, delicate
Sweet and beautiful.
Slowly, you droop
you gravitate closer
Downward.
I see you
but forget to show you the
Love and compassion you deserve.
If only you could
Reach out and
Seize all that you desire.

soar high

Hurry! catch a gust
wind stirs in a flurry, go!
take the plunge, soar High

flor

Fiery petals
dance & sway with the soft breeze
Vibrant energy

exotic in flow
erotic kiss to lips, skin
Blush of color, mine

when the sun sets

when the sun sets on us
please don't cry.
don't tell me all the reasons why
it's all my fault
I didn't try
to light your sky
forever.
what I need is time
when all rivers of love run dry
time to heal time to grow
please don't pry
when the sun sets on us...

Welcome

life on Earth is bittersweet,
lots of work and tons to eat.
No one knows just what to say,
so they set out to spend the day
trying to make things better.
we all try not to start a fight
to help keep all we're feeling light.
if you're new here, that's okay
we all stumble and lose our way
just take a breathe...
try happy

whispers of moon

Lying on the ground at night
Starting straight up at the sky
I hear a voice.
Softly it caresses flesh
Slips into mind, fearless.
Echoes of wisdom trickle through
Gravitating towards the heart
I feel it.
Whispers of moon
Guiding, trying to be heard
Healing, crying, praying
For you.
She sings a sweet song
Powerful and true
That you may someday too
Whisper songs of love to the moon.

forget me not

when my petals fall away
and she takes beauty
recall each laugh & smile shared...

(forget me not)

find me in the clouds

if you're ever looking
find me in the clouds
high in the sky
where birds sing sweetly
floating along the
wondrous colors
blending dream with reality.

www.ingramcontent.com/pod-product-compliance
Lightning Source LLC
Chambersburg PA
CBHW062112140826
49812CB00058B/1320
9789357442718